The New Day Journal

REVISED EDITION

Mauryeen O'Brien, O.P.

ACTA
ASSISTING CHRISTIANS TO ACT
PUBLICATIONS

The New Day Journal, Revised Edition
A Journey from Grief to Healing
Mauryeen O'Brien, O.P.

Edited by Gregory F. Augustine Pierce
Cover design by Tom A. Wright
Text design and typesetting by Garrison Publications

This book is dedicated to all who mourn the death of a loved one, to all who have reached out to minister to them, and to all who encouraged me to begin grief ministry–especially John F. Whealon, former Archbishop of Hartford, Carmella Jameson, my first support group facilitator, and J. William Worden, author of *Grief Counseling and Grief Therapy*.

Contents

Introduction

If you are saddened by the recent loss of a loved one, then you need to give yourself some time to work through the natural process of grieving. This book is meant to help. It is based on the premise that writing your thoughts, feelings and experiences is one of the most helpful ways to get beyond the pain caused by the death of someone you love.

In order to move on with your life after the death of another, you need to work through the four "tasks" of grieving. Part One is designed to help you do that. It is only by completing these tasks that you can eventually move on with your life, always remembering your loved one and using those memories to build your own future.

Part Two focuses on continuing the grieving process, which never really ends. It includes special sections on journeying into your new life situation and planning for the future.

The Appendixes offer suggestions for journaling around the special emotions that surround holidays after the death of your loved one and suggestions for further reading. There is also information on bereavement support groups and special prayers for you to say to help you through your grief.

The New Day Journal can be used by individuals on their own, but it can also be used by groups of people who are struggling together with sadness and loss. The Facilitator's Guide offers help to those who are leading such groups.

Some Truths About Grief

Before your begin this book it is important that you recognize several truths about the grieving process:

- Grief is a normal and natural reaction to the death of a loved one.

- Few of us are prepared for the long journey of grief that is at times devastating, frightening and lonely.

- Grief has been likened to a raw, open wound. With great care, it eventually will heal, but there will always be a scar.

- No two people grieve the same way.

- In order to move beyond your grief, you must "work" at it. There is no alternative.

- It is not selfish to be self-caring. Your loved one would have wanted you to be.

- The best therapy for your grief is to find people who will listen to you tell your "grief story" over and over.

• You should try not to make major decisions during the early stages of grief. Your judgment at that time is not as clear as it is normally.

• Grief work takes much longer than most people expect.

• Take each hour, each day, each week, each month, each year—one at a time.

The Emotions of Grief

Each person has his or her own timetable and style of grieving. Many emotions will flow from your grief work. Some people experience all of them, some just a few. No one experiences them in the same order. Which of the following emotions have you already experienced? Each of them must be faced if healing is to take place.

• disbelief/denial	• lowered self-esteem
• physical symptoms	• guilt
• idealization	• anger
• anxiety/fear	• loneliness
• bargaining	• helplessness
• depression	• preoccupation

Journal Writing

Writing in a journal, or journaling, is a good way to discover and articulate what you are going through in your grieving process. All you need to do is jot down your thoughts, feelings, anxieties, questions, etc. in the places provided in this book. Don't worry about spelling or sentence structure or quality of handwriting. Just let your pen move across the paper.

Journal keeping can also be a form of prayer. It can help you see more clearly where you have been, where you are now, and where you are heading. Journaling allows you to get an overall picture of yourself, your rhythms, your direction, and your insights into the specific events of your daily existence and their accompanying emotions.

It is important for you to begin to write what has happened to you since—and because of—the loss of your loved one. Articulating this story is a vital tool in moving yourself to the point where you can begin to heal. So, let's get started. It's a new day.

THE FOUR TASKS OF MOURNING

To Accept the Reality of the Loss

To Experience the Pain of Grief

To Adjust to an Environment in Which the Deceased Is Missing

To "Emotionally Relocate" the Deceased and Move on with Life

To Accept the Reality of the Loss

PRAYER

When Jesus arrived, he found that Lazarus had already been in the tomb four days. Now Bethany was near Jerusalem, some two miles away, and many of the Jews had come to Martha and Mary to console them about their brother. When Martha heard that Jesus was coming, she went and met him, while Mary stayed at home.

Martha said to Jesus, "Lord, if you had been here, my brother would not have died. But even now I know that God will give you whatever you ask of him."

Jesus said to her, "I am the resurrection and the life. Those who believe in me, even though they die, will live, and everyone who lives and believes in me will never die. Do you believe this?"

Martha said to him, "Yes, Lord, I believe that you are the Messiah, the Son of God, the one coming into the world."

John 11:17-27

Additional selections from Scripture:
- Job 19:1, 23-27
- Psalm 122:1-9
- Matthew 26:36-44

What Is Grief?

Grief is the process by which we adapt to any loss. The death of a loved one can be the most painful and difficult kind of grief. The process of grieving (or mourning) the death of a loved one takes different people different amounts of time, and no two people experience grief in exactly the same way.

The manifestations or effects of grief can be social (in our relations with other people), physiological (in our bodies), psychological (in our minds), and spiritual (in our souls or spirits).

Social manifestations of grief often include a change in our normal patterns of conduct. For example, we might be unable to initiate and maintain organized patterns of activity. We may exhibit restlessness, lack of concentration, even the inability to sit still around others. We can find ourselves withdrawing from or avoiding any kind of social activity.

Physiological and psychological manifestations of grief can be loss of weight, inability to sleep, crying, a tendency to sigh often, lack of strength, exhaustion, emptiness, and a feeling of heaviness or having "something stuck in the throat." Other indications of grief are heart palpitations and similar signs of anxiety such as nervousness and tension, loss of sexual desire (or, conversely, hypersexuality), lack of energy, restlessness and searching for something to do (or, conversely, apathy and sluggishness), shortness of breath, anorexia, gastrointestinal disturbances, and many others.

Spiritual manifestations of grief for some people are doubts or loss of faith, anger at God, praying for miracles or even that one's own life might end. We might become overzealous in our pieties or, conversely, refuse to pray or go to church at all.

Here is the important point about all these manifestations: they are natural, normal, not our fault, and experienced by many others. They will come and go, increase and decrease in intensity, and change often as we are going through the grieving process. Some or all of them are to be expected, and if we work through our grief using methods described in this book, most of the symptoms will decline to manageable proportions or even disappear completely.

Before we can begin the grieving process, however, we must accept the reality of the loss. "When someone dies," says Dr. J. William Worden in his book *Grief Counseling and Grief Therapy*, "even if the death has been expected, there is always a sense that it hasn't happened. The first task of grief is to believe that reunion with the person who dies will not be possible again, in this life.... Many people who have sustained a loss find themselves calling out for the lost person, and they sometimes tend to think that others who look like the person, really are the person."

The denial of a loved one's death can vary in degree, but the first reaction to the loss is a sense of unreality: "It didn't happen," "It's all a bad dream," "I'll wake up soon." Some people get stuck right here, refusing to accept the death and denying either the facts, the meaning of the death, or the irreversibility of the loss.

QUESTIONS

It is critical to our recovery that our awareness of the reality of our loss should increase gradually, both intellectually, emotionally and spiritually. Try to write down a few thoughts on the following questions in the space provided. Share your answers with someone else when and if you can.

Who has died? What was his or her relationship to you?

Who told you about it? Whom did you tell?

Were you there, or where were you when you heard?
  What was your reaction?

Where did the death occur? How did it happen?

What was the wake and funeral service like?

What was said at the service that meant a lot and you want to remember?

READING

Our Grief Journey Can Be Growth-Filled

"I don't understand God," Jean said angrily in the midst of her story about the death of her husband a year ago. "Jesus promised that whatever we ask in his name will be given to us, and I begged God to cure Bob of his cancer. I vowed a world of sacrifices. I worked at church. I volunteered at the hospital. I believed. But the Lord let me down. He didn't make Bob better."

Bob had been diagnosed with a rare type of cancer that was neither operable nor curable. Jean, a devout Catholic, prayed her husband through doctor appointments, hospital stays and treatments that left his body weak and in pain. While his body suffered, however, Bob's heart and mind had remained strong, hopeful, and filled with a buoyant spirit. Jean's prayers had taken hold of him and given him

an inner peace and joy in the midst of what he was going through.

But Bob, never someone who could put into words how he felt, had found it difficult to share what was going on inside, so his wife never knew how much her prayers had helped him. What she experienced instead was the discouraging feeling that God had not heard her prayers. "I asked for a miracle," she cried. "Why didn't God grant me my miracle?"

There is no pat and easy answer to Jean's question. When someone is grieving, it is not the time to remind him or her that God doesn't usually interfere in the natural, physical course of human events. It does no good to point out that miracles aren't just confined to bodily healing. There is no sense in reminding some-

12

one of the true miracle that somehow in death we are all united with God. Nor is it the time to tell the person that he or she will eventually be able to continue on with life. Those who grieve must be allowed to grieve; they must be permitted to experience—painful as it is—the process of grief. Otherwise, they will never overcome their grief and grow stronger.

Jean will be angry: angry at Bob for leaving her a young widow, angry at herself for not being able to prevent his death, angry at God for not performing a miracle. She may deny that Bob is really dead or pretend that it never happened. She will be depressed, and her depression will come out in all sorts of forms: lack of energy, uncontrollable tears, despair, loneliness, not caring about her own life.

Eventually, however, Jean must begin to work through a process that is as old as human history and as natural as life itself. She must grieve the loss of her husband, and in mourning his death she must choose to accept it, to close the door on it, and then begin to become actively involved in her new life. That is what this "New Day" journal is designed to help people do.

The term "work" is used purposely here, for grieving is truly work. We don't just "get over" sorrow and loss. We have to make a commitment to struggle through it. But the struggling can cause growth. There is a very beautiful book, *The Tree That Survived the Winter* by Mary Fahey. The tree of the title had to face cold and wind and snow and had to experience a certain loss of beauty before it could once again feel the warmth and life that spring brings. So it is that we who experience the death of a loved one must work out our grief before we can begin to live and grow again.

In order for anything to grow it must be nourished. We know that sunlight and water nourish a tree, but so do the storms of winter. Likewise, God nourishes us, even when life seems harsh. Many times, this nourishment comes through other people. We humans—unlike trees—have the capacity to choose whether or not we will accept such nourishment, but if we do not we will have trouble working through our grief.

The loss of someone we love can cause great bitterness and pain. Like Jean, we can turn our anger toward God. Yet sooner or later, if we work at it and accept the nourishment we are offered, we can begin to realize the truth: God doesn't take away the struggles and tragedies of life but rather journeys beside us as we go through them. Though a tree sheds its leaves in winter and appears lifeless, it is continuously taking in and storing the rays of the winter sun. In the struggle to survive, it absorbs the light and heat and reaches beyond winter to blossom into spring beauty.

A young woman who had lost her teenage son once said in utter astonishment: "You know, it's hard to believe that from all the chaos that has gone on in my life because of Billy's death I have come to feel strong. Believe me, if I could change what has happened I would, because I dearly loved my child and wanted to see him become a man. But I am a stronger person now, because I worked hard to move through my grief and to hold onto my belief in God."

Trees survive winter after winter. Some become tall, others are stunted. Some grow straight, others bent and bowed. Each is different, each survives in its own way. But in the work of surviving, all trees reach the same goal: growth! Thus all of us, as we work through our grief, will do so in our own unique ways and will come through our grief in different shapes. But the work we put in, the struggles that we endure, will produce new growth and life for us.

"I am the resurrection and the life."

On the next two pages, write the story of your loved one's death. If you prefer to type or need additional room, use additional paper and attach them to the book. Include your memories of the details of what happened and what people said to you.

_____

_____

_____

_____

_____

_____

_____

_____

_____

_____

_____

_____

_____

_____

_____

_____

_____

_____

_____

_____

_____

_____

CLOSING PRAYER

Pray the "Serenity Prayer" found on p. 84 of this book.

To Accept the Reality of the Loss

PRAYER

Jesus said, "I thank you, Father, Lord of heaven and earth, because you have hidden these things from the wise and the intelligent and have revealed them to infants; yes, Father, for such was your gracious will. All things have been handed over to me by my Father; and no one knows the Son except the Father, and no one knows the Father except the Son and anyone to whom the Son chooses to reveal him.

"Come to me, all you that are weary and are carrying heavy burdens, and I will give you rest. Take my yoke upon you, and learn from me; for I am gentle and humble in heart, and you will find rest for your souls. For my yoke is easy, and my burden is light."

Matthew 11:25-30

Additional selections from Scripture:
- Isaiah 25:6a, 7-9
- Psalm 116:5-6, 10-11, 15-16
- Matthew 5:1-12a

Working at Moving on with Our Lives

Imagine for a minute what we would be experiencing if we were on a journey for a "pearl of great price." Perhaps we are trying to become a contestant on "The Wheel of Fortune" television show, for example. Or maybe we are studying to get a college degree. Or we might be looking for the perfect apartment or building the home of our dreams. What would our journey look like? What stumbling blocks might we encounter along the way?

The journey would probably be long. Attaining fame, fortune, success, comfort and happiness usually takes awhile. Most likely, the journey would be difficult, even costly. We've learned by now that there are no "free lunches" and we never really get "something for nothing." We also know that the journey would have its own built-in obstacles along the way. No road is completely smooth.

Still, we would make the journey if we were somewhat assured that there would be a big payoff at the end of it. In the gospels, we are told that "the kingdom of heaven is like a merchant in search of fine pearls; on finding one pearl of great value, he went and sold all that he had and bought it" (Matthew 13:45-46). First the merchant journeys, then he finds what he is looking for, but then he must work and sacrifice in order to own it.

What does all this have to do with those of us who have lost a loved one? We are saddened by our loss and will continue to grieve until we make the journey to work through that grief. The journey will be long and difficult, with its own unique obstacles, but the payoff will be huge: we will be on our way to being healed.

Someone once wrote:

> A cut finger
> Is numb before it bleeds,
> It bleeds before it hurts,
> It hurts until it begins to heal,
> It forms a scab and itches until
> Finally a scar is left where
> Once there was a wound.

Grief over the death of a loved one is the deepest wound we will ever have. Like a cut finger, it will go through many stages before it finally leaves a scar. Our grief may manifest itself in anger, "bargaining" with God, disbelief, depression and many other emotions. These feelings may occur repeatedly, without any warning or order, but the thing to remember is that they're normal. They are as natural as sleeping when we are tired, eating when we are hungry, or sneezing when our nose itches. They are nature's way–God's way–of healing a broken heart.

Although our grieving may not include every single one of these emotions, they can all help us journey toward those wonderful pearls of great price: acceptance, peace and growth. But we are the ones who have to seek that treasure and be willing to sacrifice anything to possess it.

Anne, a young woman trying to come to terms with her husband's death, said to herself at least twenty times a day, "John didn't really die. It's just a bad dream." Gradually, Anne found herself acknowledging that John had died and that her life had been changed forever. "Without even realizing it," she admitted, "I began to accept that John would not be coming through the front door each night at 5:30."

Jim, a middle-aged man whose wife died after a long marriage, thought he was losing his mind when he began to have feelings he had never experienced before. "I didn't even think I was normal anymore," he explained. "I was angry and jealous of those who still had their wives. I felt guilty and lonely at the same time, over and over again."

Psychologists tell us that such feelings are neither good nor bad. They are just feelings. The task Jim has, and the task we all have in order to move on with our lives, is to name our feelings and figure out how we will handle them. We need to accept our feelings of sorrow and rage and helplessness and betrayal as part of what it means to be human. One of the biggest helps for doing this is to learn to acknowledge our feelings to ourselves and to express them to others. Hard though it is, we must experience fully, "lean into" our pain, if you will. Oh, how that hurts! And, oh, how we need to do it!

No one has to tell us how the loss of a loved one changes our world. We know because we have experienced it. In the beginning of our grief journey, we live in a transition period. During this time we need to examine what has been lost. Marie, who had been married for twenty-seven years before her husband died, acknowledged her losses this way: "You know, besides losing my husband, I've also lost some very important roles in my life. I'm no longer 'Karl's wife,' 'Karl's tennis partner,' or 'the woman who shares funny stories with Karl.' I've lost the past, but I've also lost the future."

Once Marie began to realize all of the "secondary losses" she had sustained, she was able to explore new roles that were beginning to occur in her life. She went back to school, renewed old friendships and made new ones, volunteered at her church, joined a choir and began to make the new life for herself that she knew her husband would have wanted for her.

We mourners all have new worlds to explore, new feelings to feel, new relationships to grow into. Many things have changed in our lives, but many other things remain the same. No, we will never completely get over our feelings of sadness and loss, and that's all right. But the process of grieving will result in a new "us," and that's all right too.

It won't come easily. It won't come quickly. But it will come. New life eventually came to Jim and Anne and Marie, but they had to work at it. They each had to search out their own pearl of great price, and they paid dearly for it. Once they found it, however, they were able to move on with their lives, and so will we.

QUESTIONS

If we are to find the "pearl of great price," we must begin the journey from grief to healing. Try to write down a few thoughts on the following questions in the space provided. Share your answers with someone else when and if you can.

What feelings are very strong in you at this time?

How have you handled these feelings?

What are the things about your response you'd like to change?

How have you dealt with family and friends about your grief?

What are the things you'd like to get across to them about your needs?

How are you preparing yourself for especially difficult times: birthdays, wedding anniversaries, special holidays, anniversaries of the death?

Our Feelings Are Normal

"I feel like I'm going crazy," is a statement made by many grieving people. This is because the emotions we are feeling are so raw, so uncontrolled, so painful, so new that we feel there must be something wrong with us. But these feelings are normal. Here are a few of the most common:

Sadness. This is the most common feeling manifested by people who are bereaved. Many times, crying or even uncontrolled sobbing are a part of this.

Anger. This is often experienced after a loss. It comes from two sources. First is a sense of frustration that there was nothing we could do to prevent the death. Second, we feel unable to exist without the person. Sometimes we direct our anger toward some others, even blaming them for the death. We may blame the physician or health care provider, other family members, the person who died, and often God.

Guilt. This is another common experience of many survivors. We feel guilt over not being kind enough to the deceased, not taking him or her to a doctor or hospital sooner, not being present when the person died, not foreseeing the death. Guilt is usually over something that happened or was neglected around the time of death. Most often, the guilt is irrational, but it still needs to be talked about and worked through.

Anxiety. This usually comes from two sources. First, as survivors we feel anxious that we will not be able to take care of ourselves. Second, our own awareness of mortality is heightened by the death of our loved one.

Loneliness. This feeling is frequently expressed by those who grieve, especially if they were used to a close, daily relationship with the deceased. It is not merely the physical absence of a loved one that makes us feel lonely, but rather the permanence of the loss.

Fatigue. This is a general feeling of being extremely tired all the time. The fatigue seen in people suffering from grief sometimes appears to be apathy or listlessness, but it is usually pure exhaustion from the trauma.

Shock. Shock occurs most often in the case of a sudden and unexpected death, but sometimes comes even after a long illness.

Yearning. Yearning for the lost person is a common experience and a normal response. When it starts to diminish, it may be a sign that the initial mourning period is coming to an end.

Relief. Many people feel relief after the death of a loved one, especially if the person suffered a lengthy or particularly painful illness. This, too, is a normal reaction and should not be a source of guilt.

Numbness. Right after learning of a death, we might feel numb. It is nature's way of protecting us from experiencing too many or too painful feelings all at once.

Again, all of these feelings are signs that we are going through a normal, healthy grief process. We should not deny or suppress them but rather recognize them for what they are.

(For further reading on this topic, see *Grief Counseling and Grief Therapy* by J. William Worden.)

"Come to me, all you that are weary and are carrying heavy burdens."

On the next two pages, describe the important roles your loved one had in your life. List which of them you will now have to fulfill, and how you will do each one. If you prefer to type or need more room, use additional pages and attach them to the book.

_____

_____

_____

_____

_____

_____

_____

_____

_____

_____

_____

_____

_____

_____

_____

_____

_____

_____

_____

_____

_____

_____

CLOSING PRAYER

Pray the "Serenity Prayer" found on p. 84 of this book.

TASK TWO

To Experience the Pain of Grief

PRAYER

I lift up my eyes to the hills—

>from where will my help come?

My help comes from the Lord,

>Who made heaven and earth.

He will not let your foot be moved;

>he who keeps you will not slumber.

He who keeps Israel

>will neither slumber nor sleep.

The Lord is your keeper;

>The Lord is your shade at your right hand.

The sun shall not strike you by day,

>nor the moon by night.

The Lord will keep you from all evil;

>he will keep your life.

The Lord will keep

>your going out and your coming in

>from this time on and forevermore.

Psalm 121

Additional selections from Scripture:
- Romans 8:14-23
- Lamentations 3:17-26
- John 12: 23-26

Guilt and Anger—By-Products of the Pain of Grief

Grief hurts. There is no way around this fact. We cry out for the deceased, we want to re-possess our loved one, we protest the person's permanent absence from our lives. Reality soon enough makes us aware that we need to move on. Our inability to face our pain often makes this impossible, however.

Separation of any kind causes us pain, and permanent separation causes intense pain. This pain produces feelings that often make it seem that we are out of control.

We must begin to identify and deal with these feelings. They are neither good nor bad, positive nor negative. They are merely there and must be accepted as a normal part of the grieving process. Not everyone experiences the same kind of grief or feels the pain in the same way, but we must all work through the pain one way or another.

Don't listen to people who tell you, "Don't show your feelings" or "Get yourself so busy you can't think or feel" or "Take a trip to forget your emotions." Hard as it is, we need to let the pain of our grief hit us full force at the time of our loved one's death. Otherwise we will carry it with us for the rest of our lives.

There are always some feelings of guilt after the death of a loved one. Could we have done more to make sure the person took care of his or her health? Should we have gotten him or her to a doctor or hospital sooner? A long illness may have led to feelings of resentment toward the person, and consequently we feel badly about that. A sudden or accidental death may have given rise to feelings of "if only I had...." The ultimate guilt may come from a suicide. Friends or family may blame us for the person's action, or we may blame ourselves.

These feelings of guilt are normal, but we all need to meet them head on. If there is some-thing we should feel guilty about, we need to forgive ourselves and seek the forgiveness of others–even our loved one who has died. We might need to face our guilt on a spiritual level and ask God's forgiveness. Sometimes our guilt may be more than we can handle alone. It often helps to talk about our feelings with friends and relatives, and we should consider seeking professional help if we cannot overcome these feelings.

More than likely, however, whatever guilt we feel comes merely from the fact that we are human beings and not perfect. We cannot control the actions of others or what happens to them. We can only love them and love ourselves.

Anger is another strong but normal reaction to the pain of grief. Depending on our personality and the circumstances of the death of our loved one, we may experience anger in varying degrees. We may be angry at the doctors and nurses for not saving our loved one. If there was an accident, we might be angry at the one who caused it or at our loved one for being careless. We may be angry with God: "What kind of God would let this happen?" or "Why did God let this happen to me?"

We need to express this anger, and we can do so in many ways: screaming, crying, hard exercise, beating on something, writing, talking to someone. No matter what form of expression is used, however, we need to get our anger out and not keep it stuffed inside.

Anger will come and go, and there is nothing wrong with it. We do need to work out a way to express it that is healthy for us and socially acceptable, but not to express it can be harmful to ourselves and to others.

(For further reading on this topic, see *Grief Counseling and Grief Therapy* by J. William Worden.)

QUESTIONS

Pain, guilt, anger are all a natural part of the healing process. Try to write down a few thoughts on the following questions in the space provided. Share your answers with someone else when and if you can.

What are the various ways you hurt because of the death of your loved one?

How do you try to avoid or deny the pain?

What have others told you to do about your grief? How has their advice been helpful or harmful?

Name any reasons you might be suffering from guilt regarding the death of your loved one. Include people who are making you feel guilty, even if they are unaware of it.

How might you overcome these feelings?

How have you expressed your anger over the death of your loved one?

Have you been angry with God? Why? What are you going to do about it?

READING

Emotions That Surface after Someone We Love Dies

Grief is an integral part of the human response to any loss, especially the death of a loved one. When we grieve, many of our human emotions are intensified.

In her classic book, *On Death and Dying,* Elizabeth Kubler-Ross describes five stages that are present in the grieving process: denial, anger, bargaining, resignation/depression and accep-

tance. It is important to understand that these five stages are normal and healthy, but also that it is necessary to work through them if we want to heal our grief. These reactions occur over and over and usually never in order. Some people experience all of them, some just a few.

Denial usually centers on not wanting to let go of the person who died. "No, this can't be happening to me," we cry. The opposite of denial is telling everyone that we are fine, being stoic, not showing our emotions. But in fact we need to tell the story of our beloved's death over and over so that we can hear ourselves acknowledge that the person has really died and hear our own sadness.

Another form of denial is our refusal to admit our own mortality. The death of a loved one forces us to face the inevitability of our own death before we can accept that of another.

Anger is primarily a feeling of helplessness. "What did I do to deserve this?" we ask ourselves. Anger can be directed at many people: the person who dies, the health care providers, God, ourselves, those who still have a spouse, children, parent, etc.

We often have an inability when we are grieving to express how "mad" we are, but we need to get our anger out into the open and share it with others. Certainly, we must learn to deal with our anger constructively, but suppressing it is not the answer. Rage is a healthy, normal, human response to death.

When we grieve, we try to "bargain" our way out of the reality of our situation with many "if onlys." "If only I had made my husband go to the doctor (or take his pills or stay in bed)." "If only my wife had retired." "If only our son hadn't driven at night."

We even try to bargain retroactively with God. "If only you hadn't taken my beloved, I would have...." Life and death are the result of many uncontrollable forces, and the "if onlys" cannot change them.

Another stage of grieving is resignation, which can turn into depression unless we go through the complete mourning process. Because if we haven't mourned completely, we can turn bitterly inward upon ourselves.

There are many mood swings to the grieving process. If we work at it, however, the "down" ones gradually become fewer and less severe, the "up" ones last longer and are more frequent.

Finally, we arrive at the stage of acceptance. "Yes, this has happened and I am very sad, but my life has not stopped or ended and my loved one would want me to continue and be happy."

Acceptance means beginning to live in the present, remembering the good of the past and looking forward in anticipation to the future. It includes learning to take one day at a time, to express how we feel, to have more confidence in ourselves. We come to accept the person who died as a whole person, someone who was good and at times not so good. We create for ourselves some "cherishable memories" of the deceased that we can take with us into the future.

Acceptance means accepting our own humanity and mortality. It is what allows us to begin to make or renew relationships and friendships apart from our loved one. It only comes if and when we work through the tasks of grief.

The process of working through these tasks will take a long time. It cannot happen overnight. Once one task has been worked through, we may find that we slip back and need to work at it again. We often hear that "time heals all things." This may be true, but it is *what we do with the time* that really matters.

(For further reading on this topic, see *On Death and Dying* by Elizabeth Kubler-Ross.)

"I lift up my eyes to the hills—from where will my help come?"

What emotions are you feeling most strongly since your loved one has died? On the next two pages, describe these feelings and what stage you are at in working through them. If you prefer to type or need additional room, use additional pages and attach them to the book.

_____

_____

_____

_____

_____

_____

_____

_____

_____

_____

_____

_____

_____

_____

_____

_____

_____

_____

_____

_____

_____

_____

_____

CLOSING PRAYER

Pray the "Serenity Prayer" found on p. 84 of this book.

To Experience the Pain of Grief

PRAYER

I will extol you, my God and King,
   and bless your name forever and ever.

Every day I will bless you,
   and praise your name forever and ever.

The Lord is good to all
   and his compassion is over all that he has made.

The Lord is faithful in all his words,
   and gracious in all his deeds.

The Lord upholds all who are falling,
   and raises up all who are bowed down.

My mouth will speak the praise of the Lord,
   and all flesh will bless his holy name forever and ever.

Psalm 145:1-2, 9, 13b-14, 21

Additional selections from Scripture
   • Daniel 12:1-3
   • John 6:51-59
   • Romans 6:3-9

REFLECTION

The Loneliness of Grief

One of the main feelings frequently expressed by those who grieve, especially if they were used to a close, day-to-day relationship with the deceased, is loneliness. There is a simple loneliness that comes from not having a friend and companion with whom to share a meal or a holiday. There is also the loneliness of panic that occurs when misfortune strikes and we must suddenly face a crisis alone, sometimes for the first time in many years.

Loneliness is not only experienced by those who grieve, however. Many people who are away from their families or who have few friends speak of periods of loneliness, but it is the permanence of the absence that makes the pain of our loneliness following the death of a loved one so severe and long-lived. Such loneliness can come upon us when we least expect it. A common experience, for example, is to think of something to say to our loved one and he or she is not there to respond. The loneliness of grief is filled with special sadness because we cannot change the permanence or the absoluteness of it.

There is a difference between loneliness and aloneness. Both are choices made by the individual, but loneliness can be very painful and destructive, while aloneness can be a positive, life-giving experience.

Loneliness is often merely an unconscious, self-imposed isolation, while aloneness can be a choice that has been well thought out. People who are lonely often have a fear of risking social situations without someone by their side to "protect" them. People who choose to be alone (after the death of a spouse, for example) are looking for the freedom and the time to better themselves or pursue their own interests.

Lonely people will blame others for not seeking them out, while people who are alone realize that they can reach out to others at any time and do so whenever they feel the need. Being alone can force us to learn our own self-worth as measured by our personal value system, while loneliness feels incomplete without another's input. The lonely think that they are boring and undesirable, but the alone know they are interesting to themselves and therefore assume that they are interesting to others.

You will find that people who choose loneliness have underdeveloped skills in divergent thinking and are too secure with old habits to try anything new. Those who choose to be alone, on the other hand, are willing to experiment with new thoughts and activities and use creative thinking to solve their problems. The lonely feel that they are being controlled by circumstances or that only another person could remedy their situation, while the alone are in control of what happens to them. Likewise, those who are alone accept full accountability for their actions, while those who are lonely fear assuming responsibility for much of anything.

The lonely choose to feel miserable rather than make themselves vulnerable. They also feel at some level that they do not deserve the interest and even the love of others. Those who are alone realize that such feelings are self-generated. Their egos are healthy enough to know that they are loved and lovable—even when they are not "with" others. They are willing to reach out to others, even while they accept the risk that they might be hurt.

Obviously, any individual person is not all one way or all the other. Nobody is "perfectly lonely" or "perfectly alone." Still, it is a useful exercise to determine which way we lean after the death of a loved one and then to decide how we really want to be in our grieving process.

(For further reading on this topic, see *Grief Counseling and Grief Therapy* by J. William Worden.)

QUESTIONS

Are you lonely after the death of a loved one, or are you alone? Try to write down a few thoughts on the following questions in the space provided. Share your answers with someone else when and if you can.

Describe a time when you wanted to share something with your deceased loved one. How did you feel?

What are your loneliest times?

Is it helpful to be alone, at least at times? Explain.

Do you think that you are a person people want to be around? Why or why not?

Who are the people to whom you can now turn for companionship whenever you want or need to do so?

Choose to Be Alone

We are geared to be a social society; the "loner" is a misfit to be pitied. For a person to choose or to accept being alone seems to make others uncomfortable. We often judge the person to be "odd" or "strange."

Feelings of loneliness seem to hit us especially hard after the loss of a significant person in our lives. If we could use those times of aloneness to aid the healing process, the healing might come sooner, because being alone can allow us to experience the pain and sort out the buried emotions without distraction. Being alone provides the opportunity–and the challenge–to distinguish the important from the trivial, the valuable from the worthless.

The following are suggestions for dealing with loneliness and for making aloneness productive.

After a loved one has died, those of us left behind often feel most lonely in the most familiar environments, such as our homes. To change that negative feeling to a positive, go into your house and act as if you have just walked into a stranger's home for the first time. Pick out all the delightful things to look at. Next, look for a project to work on–for example, something to clean out, rearrange or change to add a little more cheer to the environment. You would do it for a friend; do it for yourself!

Darkness tends to isolate us and causes great feelings of loneliness for many. Try to begin to appreciate the dark, the moonlight, the stars, the night sounds, the slowing down of the body and daily activities. Think of new things you can do in the evening before bed to break up the routine that perpetuates your loneliness. If television is your habit, turn it off. Read, think, plan the next day's activities, write letters, call someone else who might be lonely, call someone whom you have never called.

Holidays are problem times for most of us who are grieving. Even people not prone to loneliness or who are involved in many activities tend to feel some isolation during the holidays. Try to be alone for at least one hour of each holiday to set your priorities in order and to appreciate what you have, including your fond and rich memories of your loved one.

Weather affects the emotions of many who grieve. Some dark, dreary day–when you know you usually would feel lonely–choose instead to "be alone." Think of what you would like to have someone do for you, then do it for yourself or for someone else. Spend your time writing a letter or baking or making something for a specific person. Do something easy that can be completed in one day, and at the end of the day or the next morning deliver it.

The important point of these experiments is that rather than "being lonely" you choose to "be alone." When you feel in command of this situation, you will feel very powerful to make other wise decisions. Friedrich Nietzsche said, "Solitude makes us tougher toward ourselves and more tender towards others."

Don't set limits on the length of time you choose to be alone. Stick with it as long as it is helpful and enjoyable. Then in the future, when you begin to feel lonely, try to remember this experiment and recreate the feelings.

(Adapted from an article by Tiaynah Ann Mikol.)

JOURNALING

"The Lord upholds all who are falling, and raises up all who are bowed down."

There are many times when you feel sad and lonely because of the death of a loved one. On the next two pages, describe how these feelings impact your daily life and how you are dealing with them—successfully or unsuccessfully. If you prefer to type or need more room, use additional pages and attach them to the book.

_____

_____

_____

_____

_____

_____

_____

_____

_____

_____

_____

_____

_____

_____

_____

_____

_____

_____

_____

_____

_____

_____

_____

_____

CLOSING PRAYER

Pray the "Serenity Prayer" found on p. 84 of this book.

To Adjust to an Environment in Which the Deceased Is Missing

PRAYER

God of Life,

There are days when the burdens we carry
chafe our shoulders and wear us down,
when the road seems dreary and endless,
the skies gray and threatening,
when our lives have no music in them,
and our hearts are lonely,
and our souls have lost their courage.

Flood the path with light,
we beseech thee Lord.

Turn our eyes
to where the heavens are full of promise.

St. Augustine

Additional selections from Scripture:

- 2 Maccabees 12:43-46
- Luke 23:33, 39-43
- Romans 5:5-11

REFLECTION

It's a New Day

The loss of a loved one forever changes our world. It's a new place for us personally and socially—a place where the deceased is no longer present. Because an ending has occurred, new beginnings must and will take place. It is a new day, whether we look forward to it or not.

Before we can move on, however, a period of transition will take place. When the first two tasks of grieving have been worked through—when we have accepted the reality of the loss and allowed ourselves to experience the pain of grief—then we must begin to adjust to an environment in which the deceased is missing.

During this period of time, we need to examine closely what has been lost as well as what has been found. Some things have changed, others continue the same. There are experiences, roles, expectations, values, opportunities and dreams to be given up, but there are new ones to be begun or taken up.

In addition to the primary loss of our loved one, there are many secondary losses that follow as a result. We need to identify each of these and grieve each one. Appropriate ways of achieving closure on these secondary losses must be sought out.

How long and how well we adjust to our new environment depends in large part on our relationship with the deceased and the various roles he or she played in our life. For example, our loved one may have been companion, accountant, gardener, baby sitter, friend, tennis partner, car mechanic, cook, parent, bridge partner, etc.

Many of us resent having to develop new skills or find new people to take on roles that were formerly performed by our loved one, but people who do not face up to the task of adjusting most probably will remain stuck in their grief. By not developing the skills and relationships we need to cope with new realities, we are working against ourselves and promoting our own helplessness.

Ultimately, we need to redefine our life goals in a world we do not want and perhaps could never imagine: a world from which our loved one is absent. That is our new responsibility as survivors.

(For further reading on this topic, see *Grief Counseling and Grief Therapy* by J. William Wordon.)

QUESTIONS

Recently-bereaved people are discouraged from making major life-changing decisions because they are not ready. Eventually, however, these issues must be faced. Try to write down a few thoughts on the following questions in the space provided. Share your answers with someone else when and if you can.

What are some things that you need to decide right away? List a few people who can help you make the decisions.

What are some of the decisions that you need to put off for a while? Why?

Which of the roles that your loved one performed in your life will you miss the most?

Which of those roles do you now need to take on yourself? How do you feel about them?

Who can possibly take on some of your loved one's other roles? When and how can they begin to do so?

How do you feel about continuing on without your love one? What would he or she have wanted you to do?

Why the Grieving Process Lasts So Long

It is often difficult for the family, friends and colleagues of a person who has experienced the loss of a loved one to understand why the grieving process lasts so long. They want to see us happy again and "getting on with life." It is therefore important to be aware of the many kinds and levels of loss that can accompany the death of a loved one. This awareness may help us—and others who care about us—to be more patient and more gentle to ourselves and to others during the grieving process.

In addition to the obvious and overwhelming loss of our loved one, we will often experience other "secondary losses" as well:

Loss of a Large Part of Ourselves. There is always a part of ourselves that was given to our loved one in a special way. This chunk of ourselves is gone now, too.

Loss of Identity. Part of who we are includes what we did with and for the other person. This part of ourselves can seem to be violently wrenched from our very being when a loved one dies.

Loss of Self-Confidence. The feeling of inadequacy—of not being able to do anything right—is often very strong after the death of a loved one. A grieving person doesn't always recognize his or her strength or wholeness.

Loss of a Chosen Lifestyle. Death forces us to begin a new lifestyle, whether we want to or not. For example, a person who has chosen to be married is suddenly forced to be single again. It is this sense of being forced into the situation that is so difficult.

Loss of Security. When a loved one dies, we lose even the most basic sense of security. We don't know what will happen next or how we will respond emotionally or how we should react in social situations. If the loved one was a parent or spouse, we might also suffer from financial hardship or insecurity.

Loss of Feeling Safe. When death takes a loved one, we feel exposed to the harsh winds of life. We are vulnerable as we have never been before, and we perceive our own mortality in a whole new way.

Loss of Family Structure. All families form a system. This system—which is often unrecognized and unnamed—is instantly changed by a death. These changes can create adjustments among survivors that must be faced and worked out. For example, if a child dies—no matter at what age—or if a parent dies—no matter what age the children might be—a whole new set of relationships within the family must be developed.

Loss of the Past. When a loved one dies, he or she takes a history away that we do not share exactly with any other person. While new or renewed friends and acquaintances can be very supportive and accepting, they do not share the sense of our past journey the way only our deceased loved one could.

Loss of the Future. Whereas with our loved one we may have felt very comfortable facing the future, without him or her it is often frightening to think ahead to next week or next month or next year. We also fear that our future will be as painful as our present.

Loss of Direction. We can feel that our life doesn't seem to have a purpose, that nothing seems to matter anymore.

Loss of Dreams. All of our plans can disappear in a moment with the death of a loved one. We must learn to mourn the loss of those dreams and to dream new ones.

Loss of Trust. The deep levels of loss and insecurity we feel can make it very difficult to even trust ourselves–much less others–for a long period of time. Part of the grieving process is to begin to take the risk of being hurt again.

Loss of Sharing. Depending on how close the loved one was to us, we can experience the loss of a friend or confidant with whom we could share our inmost thoughts and feelings. We suddenly have no one who listens to the big events (and little nothings) of our daily existence.

Loss of Focus. The death of a loved one can affect us so strongly that we cannot focus on the day-to-day tasks of life that now seem to be "frivolous" or "non-essential."

Loss of Control. Because of the change that has been forced upon us, we conclude that we have no control over our life and that whatever choices we make are irrelevant or meaningless.

Loss of Decision-Making Ability. Grieving people often ask others, "What should I do?" Then we become even more confused because everyone gives us a different answer. This leads us to question our own ability to make decisions for ourselves.

Loss of Humor, Happiness, Joy. The sadness of death and the loss of one of the most important people in our life usually makes it very difficult for us to experience humor. Nothing seems funny, and it seems somehow wrong that we should feel any sense of happiness or joy.

Loss of Patience with Self. We can feel inadequate when our feelings of grief last for a long period of time. Even though the normal initial grieving period for most people after the loss of a close loved one is two to five years, we expect to feel better immediately and we regret the pain and trouble our grieving causes others.

Loss of Health. This is perhaps the most obvious and most dangerous secondary loss of all. We can experience everything from physical ailments, including nausea, migraine headaches, muscle knots, and back problems to psychological or spiritual afflictions such as depression or loss of faith.

There are other kinds of secondary losses that we can experience that are not on this list, and not everyone experiences each secondary loss at the same level of intensity. Still, the list helps us understand why the grieving process takes so long and why nothing can replace it. If we are to move beyond our grief, we must admit, confront and overcome each of our losses. It takes time for these wounds to form scars, for the darkness of grief to give way to the light of life.

"There are days when the burdens we carry chafe our shoulders."

Look over the list on pp. 42-43 of "secondary losses" that people experience after the death of a loved one. On the next two pages, choose the five most significant losses you have felt and describe how you feel about each one and what you think you can do to overcome them. If you prefer to type or need more room, use additional pages and attach them to the book.

_____

_____

_____

_____

_____

_____

_____

_____

_____

_____

_____

_____

_____

_____

_____

_____

_____

_____

_____

_____

_____

_____

CLOSING PRAYER

Pray the "Serenity Prayer" found on p. 84 of this book.

TASK THREE
(CONTINUED)

To Adjust to an Environment in Which the Deceased Is Missing

PRAYER

We seem to give our loved ones back to you, Lord.
You gave them to us.
But just as you did not lose them in giving,
neither do we lose them in return.

You don't give in the same way that the world gives.
What you give you don't take away.
You have taught us that what is yours is ours also,
if we are yours.

Life is eternal, Lord, and your love is undying.
And death is only a horizon.
And a horizon is nothing
but the limits of our sight.

Lift us, strong, Son of God, that we may see farther.
Cleanse our eyes that we may see more clearly,
Draw us closer to yourself, that we may find ourselves
Closer to our loved ones who are with you.

And while you prepare a place for them,
prepare us also for that happy place
where you are
and where we hope to be...forever.

(author unknown)

Additional selections from Scripture:
- Psalm 143:1-2, 5-10
- Isaiah 41:8-10
- Mark 16: 1-16

REFLECTION

From Survival to Growth

Surviving the death of a loved one is not enough. It is not enough for ourselves, for we deserve to live the fullest life of which we are capable. It is not enough for our friends and relatives, who need us to be fully and completely present to them. It is not enough for our deceased loved one, who certainly would want us to be happy. And it is not enough for God, who wants us to continue to live.

In order to move from survival to growth, however, we must first survive. That means that we have to accept the reality of the loss and experience the pain of grief. The more we loved the departed, the longer this may take. Still, we must know and believe that we will get better, that tomorrow will come if we can just move through today.

In the early stages of grief, we must be gentle with ourselves. We should stick to a simple schedule (especially on Sundays, holidays and anniversaries), avoid big decisions, cry and be comforted, seek and accept the support of others, and realize that we are not alone in our grief. We shouldn't be afraid to cherish keepsakes of our loved one if they help us mourn.

This is the time to stay close to God. As we begin to heal, we need to continue to be gentle with ourselves. It's okay to feel sadness, guilt, anger, loneliness—these are all normal emotions—for an extended period of time.

We should take care of ourselves as we grieve. We must keep eating to build up our strength, and not turn to smoking, drugs, or alcohol for relief. If the deceased was a spouse or "significant other," we should be careful not to begin a serious relationship too soon. We have to allow ourselves time to heal, and we cannot let anyone rush us.

Growth will begin to happen as we begin to adjust to an environment in which the deceased is missing. We start by looking for the good in ourselves. We meet new people and reconnect with old friends. We begin new and rekindle old interests. We look for groups or things that help us move towards self-knowledge and self-improvement.

We regain our sense of appreciation for life. We try to be creative, enjoy our freedom to choose, and choose to be happy. We start new traditions. We even begin to do things for others—including those who have just lost a loved one themselves.

Will we ever get over completely the loss of our loved one? No, thank God. Will our world ever be exactly the same without them? Obviously not. But can we continue on with our lives, without feeling guilty or being overwhelmed by sadness? Yes, we can, with God's help.

QUESTIONS

If we are to move from survival to growth, we must begin to adjust to life without our loved one. We can either do so grudgingly and ineffectively, or we can do so with a sense of hope and openness and healing. Try to write down a few thoughts on the following questions in the space provided. Share your answers with someone else when and if you can.

Who are some of the people who have helped you through your grief? How can you reconnect with them in order to grow?

What plan or project would your loved one want you to undertake? Describe it and how you might begin to make it a reality.

What is the good in yourself? How can you make it grow?

Is there some group or activity that you can join that you might enjoy? How will you find out about it and when will you join?

Who needs you to do something for them? How will you start?

READING

There Is Hope

Various dictionaries define "to hope" as "to cherish a desire with expectations of fulfillment," "to long for with expectations of attainment," and "to expect with desire." There are strong words for the grieving contained in these definitions: "cherish," "desire," "expect," "fulfillment," "attainment."

Somehow, despite all the pain and sorrow that we've gone through over the death of a loved one, we find that there remains within us a semblance of hope. There has to be, or we could not go on. "Were it not for hope, the heart would break," says the proverb.

There is a story in the gospels of a woman who had been suffering from a hemorrhage for twelve years, yet she still "expected with desire" to be healed by Jesus. She says simply, "If I but touch his clothes, I will be made well" (Mark 5:28). There was also a "desire with expectations of fulfillment" in the "good thief," who pleaded from his own cross at the most hopeless moment of his life, "Jesus, remember me when you come into your kingdom" (Luke 23:42). In both of these cases, the hope was fulfilled. Against all odds and conventional wisdom, the woman was cured, the thief was promised paradise.

Charles Peguy, a French writer who lived in the 1800s, had the wonderful ability to write as if God was speaking the lines. Here are the words that he puts in the mouth of God in his book, *God Speaks:* "My hope is the bloom, and the fruit, and the leaf, and the limb, and the twig, and the shoot, and the seed, and the bud. Hope is the shoot and the bud of the bloom of eternity itself."

Is there any hope left in us? Yes, there is. It may be small, fragile, hidden—"the shoot and the bud of the bloom of eternity itself." We may even feel a little guilty about holding on to it. But without it our hearts would break. Let us continually, unrelentlessly, unreasonably cherish our desire not only to survive the loss of our loved one, not even to heal from it, but to grow because of it.

"We seem to give our loved ones back to you, Lord."

Where are you now on your grief journey? You have survived, but how are you healing? On the next two pages, write some of the evidences of growth in your life. If you prefer to type or need more room, use additional pages and attach them to the book.

_____

_____

_____

_____

_____

_____

_____

_____

_____

_____

_____

_____

_____

_____

_____

_____

_____

_____

_____

_____

_____

_____

_____

_____

CLOSING PRAYER

Pray the "Serenity Prayer" found on p. 84 of this book.

To "Emotionally Relocate" the Deceased and Move on with Life

PRAYER

Dear Lord, I know that...

To *let go* is not to welcome sorrow but learn from it.

To *let go* is not to deny but to accept.

To *let go* is not to stop caring but to care in a different way.

To *let go* is not to reject what was but to make the most of what can be.

To *let go* is not to isolate myself but to realize I can make it on my own.

To *let go* is not to push others away but to let them into my life.

To *let go* is not to forget the past but to live in the present and dream for the future.

To *let go* is to fear less and love more.

Dear Lord, help me to *let go*.

(author unknown)

Additional selections from Scripture:
   • Psalm 34:1-10
   • Luke 7:11-17
   • Romans 14:7-8

REFLECTION

How Can I Go On?

If we are to succeed in working through the process of grief and moving on with our life, we have to find a way to find a new place in our lives or emotions for our lost loved one. We call this "emotionally relocating" the deceased. This does not mean that we forget the person. That is neither possible nor desirable. Rather, we need to find a special place to keep him or her alive in a real way. "Relocating" the deceased give us the permission we need to live with our loss and continue to move through life in a healthy, love-filled way, knowing where the person is and where we can find him or her when we need or want to.

This "emotional relocation" involves creating some cherishable memories of the person who is now physically gone but is still alive in spirit. We need to begin a "remembering process" by actively reviving and reviewing the stories of our relationship to our loved one—from beginning to end, including the good and the not-so-good. These memories can be thought, prayed about, written down, but they also need to be spoken aloud to others. The telling may be painful, but in the telling the stories are transformed into images capable of becoming part of our very being. Only then can the bonds that attach us to the other person (not the attachment itself) be loosened enough so that they do not hold us back from living our life productively.

Once we have relocated our loved one firmly in our hearts, we can form a new relationship with him or her—one that will last forever, one that no other relationship can erase. We can begin to remember our beloved without the searing pain we once had. We can begin to realize that the deceased will not be loved less because we are capable of loving ourselves and others.

Grieving is a long-term process. We can't set a definite date for its completion. Different people mourn at different rates and in different ways. Many say that we need to go through at least the seasons of a full year before grief can even begin to subside, and most people take two to five years before they feel they are beginning to complete the process.

That process includes accepting the reality of our loss, experiencing the pain of our grief, adjusting to an environment in which the deceased is missing, and finally "emotionally relocating" our loved one to a new place no one else will ever take. Only when we have accomplished these four tasks will we be able to continue on with our lives the way our loved one would surely want us to do.

(For further reading on this topic, see *Grief Counseling and Grief Therapy* by J. William Worden.)

QUESTIONS

Your loved one must continue to exist, but in a new place in your life or emotions. It is up to you to create that place and "relocate" your loved one there. Try to write down a few thoughts on the following questions in the space provided. Share your answers with someone else when and if you can.

What were some of the good stories of your relationship with your loved one?

What were some of the not-so-good stories?

How will you go about creating "cherishable memories" of your loved one?

Who can you share these memories with?

Describe the place in your heart where your loved one will reside.

Will you visit that place often? What will you say?

Letting Go and Letting God

How often have I heard the words, "Let go and let God"? It seems that whenever I am faced with a crisis or an obstacle or a loss in my life, someone is there to quote those words to me. But sometimes I wonder: What do they really mean? Just what does it mean to "let go," and how do I "let God"?

The Book of Ecclesiastes reminds us, "For everything there is a season, and a time for every matter under heaven" (3:10), and there is "a time to keep and a time to throw away" (3:6). But for me the difficulty comes from knowing what the appropriate time is in each situation. In a way, "letting go and letting God" is easier said than done. Sometimes the choice brings me satisfaction and contentment, but there are other times when things don't work out and my life goes in a direction I hadn't expected. It's at that precise time, however, that I find I must loosen my grip, step back, and really "let go and let God."

My model for this is Mary, the mother of Jesus. How many times in her life did she "let go and let God." First, there is the remarkable story of the Annunciation. What if Mary had insisted on keeping control instead of saying "let it be with me according to your word" (Luke 1:38)? Would the Incarnation ever have occurred?

Then, at the very beginning of Jesus' life, Mary was faced with losing him. A simple trip to the Passover festival ends with a disaster that would devastate any parent. When her twelve-year-old son was finally found, however, he gave her no solace. "Why were you searching for me? Did you not know I must be in my Father's house?" (Luke 2:49). Mary was left to "let go and let God," and all she could do was treasure "all these things in her heart" (Luke 2: 51).

Finally, at Calvary, Mary was faced with the ultimate tragedy: her son crucified on a cross in the prime of his life, his work a seeming failure. She had to once again "let go and let God," and she did.

I know a woman who has a plaque on her kitchen wall that says simply: "Whatever!" She has learned that the best way to hang on is to let God's strength work through her. "When I try to control everything," she explains, "I often put energy into the wrong solution. But letting go of my own will allows God to communicate with me. I learn where God would like me to be." This woman's "Whatever!" is a short prayer, but the simplicity of it allows her to work through her difficult situations using God's strength rather than her own.

Certainly, the process of letting go is painful. In a way we've all been raised with the attitude that we can and should control things. But in reality, bad things do happen—even to "good" people. The acceptance of that fact does not mean that we should forget what happened or pretend that it doesn't hurt, but in letting go of our grief we can say good-bye to one dream and begin to design another. And letting God help us design that new dream can be a powerful thing.

As one young woman whose father died said to me, "It doesn't mean I love my father less when I can open my heart to other people."

One of the greatest helps in healing my own grief over the death of loved ones has been to reach out to others in pain. I honor the dead by remembering them and using those memories to make me strong. With that strength I can then reach out to others who are hurting. It is only in "letting go and letting God" that I have become open to healing and growth, and in that healing and growth process I have begun to remember my loved ones without the wrenching pain I once felt.

"To let go is not to forget the past but to live in the present."

What specific "cherishable memories" of your loved one do you want to hold onto for the rest of your life? On the next two pages, write some of these memories, allowing them to become part of you forever. If you prefer to type or need more room, use additional pages and attach them to the book.

_____

_____

_____

_____

_____

_____

_____

_____

_____

_____

_____

_____

_____

_____

_____

_____

_____

_____

_____

_____

_____

_____

_____

CLOSING PRAYER

Pray the "Serenity Prayer" found on p. 84 of this book.

CONTINUING THE GRIEVING PROCESS

JOURNEYING TOWARD NEW LIFE

MOVING TOWARD CLOSURE

Journeying toward New Life

PRAYER

One night a man had a dream. He dreamed that he was walking along the beach with the Lord. Across the sky flashed scenes from his life. In each scene, he noticed footprints in the sand—some belonging to him and the others to the Lord.

When the last scene of his life flashed before him, he looked back at the footprints in the sand. He noticed that many times along the path of his life, at the very lowest and saddest times in his life, there was only one set of footprints.

This really bothered the man, and he questioned the Lord about it. "Lord, you said that once I decided to follow you, you'd walk with me all the way. But I have noticed that during the most troublesome times of my life, there was only one set of footprints. I don't understand why, when I needed you most, you would leave me."

The Lord replied, "My precious child, I love you and I would never leave you. During your times of trial and suffering, when you see only one set of prints, it was then I carried you."

(author unknown)

Additional selections from Scripture:

- Psalm 139:1-18
- Isaiah 43:1b-2, 4a, 5a
- Mark 14:32-42

The Road to Emmaus

The first thing that we must understand is that God has not caused our suffering. Rabbi Harold Kushner, who lost a young son in death, struggled long and hard with the question: "Why did God let my son die?" He writes of this struggle throughout his famous book, *When Bad Things Happen to Good People.* Toward the end of the book, Kushner concludes:

God does not cause our misfortunes. Some are caused by bad luck, some are caused by bad people, and some are simply an inevitable natural law. The painful things that happen to us are not punishments for our misbehavior, nor are they in any way part of some grand design on God's part. Because the tragedy is not God's will, we need not feel hurt or betrayed by God when tragedy strikes. We can turn to him for help in overcoming it, precisely because we can tell ourselves that God is as outraged by it as we are.

It is by turning to God, in fact, that we can move along on our journey of grief. No one was killed more unjustly than Jesus, who was God's own son. But God's response to Jesus' death was not to explain it or to punish those who killed him or to wipe out those who allowed it. God's response was to transform that tragic event into the greatest miracle of all, the Resurrection, that extends to all of us the capacity to regain what we have lost.

Jesus' human capacities were stretched beyond limit by his ordeal (just as ours are when we face our own death or suffering or that of a loved one). In the Garden of Gethsemane, Jesus begged God, "Abba, Father, for you all things are possible; remove this cup from me" (Mark 14:36). How many times do we pray for the same thing, much like Christ?

Jesus agonized so much that his sweat was like drops of blood. He was fully human in that garden, before he began his journey to Calvary. If Jesus can feel sadness and doubt, why can't we?

But there are many events in the gospels that show us that Christ's journey was transformed from grief into healing and growth. For example, do you remember the story of the two disciples on their way to Emmaus right after Jesus had died? They were confused and sad, truly in mourning for their friend—so much so that they never recognized the risen Christ when he approached them on their walk. Listen to their story:

Now on that same day two of them were going to a village called Emmaus, about seven miles from Jerusalem, and talking with each other about all these things that had happened. While they were talking and discussing, Jesus himself came near and went with them, but their eyes were kept from recognizing him. And he said to them, "What are you discussing with each other while you walk along?"

They stood still, looking sad. Then one of them, whose name was Cleopas, answered him, "Are you the only stranger in Jerusalem who does not know the things that have taken place there in these days?"

He asked them, "What things?" They replied, "The things about Jesus of Nazareth, who was a prophet mighty in deed and word before God and all the people, and how our chief priests and leaders handed him over to be condemned to death and crucified him. But we had hoped that he was the one to redeem Israel. Yes, and besides all this, it is now the third day since these things took place. Moreover, some women of our group astounded us. They were at the tomb early this morning, and when they did not find his body there, they came back and told us that they had indeed seen a vision of angels who said that he was alive. Some of those who were with us went to the tomb and found it just as the women had said; but they did not see him."

Then he said to them, "Oh, how foolish you are, and how slow of heart to believe all that the prophets have declared! Was it not necessary that the Messiah should suffer these things and then enter into his glory?" Then beginning with Moses and all the prophets, he interpreted to them the things about himself in all the scriptures.

As they came near the village to which they were going, he walked ahead as if he were going on. But they urged him strongly, saying, "Stay with us, because it is almost evening and the day is now nearly over." So he went in to stay with them. When he was at the table with them, he took bread, blessed and broke it, and gave it to them. Then their eyes were opened, and they recognized him; and he vanished from their sight. They said to each other, "Were not our hearts burning within us while he was talking to us on the road, while he was opening the scriptures to us?" (Luke 24:13-30).

There are many things to notice about this story. See how it took time for these two disciples to mourn the loss of their friend. Their grief journey from Jerusalem to Emmaus was seven miles—symbolizing a long one. Clearly, the were depressed and angry and had not yet reached the stage of accepting Jesus' death.

Notice, too, how Jesus invites them to tell their sad tale of loss. It was only after they had finished recounting the events surrounding their grief that they could hear what Jesus had to say. Only then were they ready to see the risen Christ in the breaking of the bread. Later, the two would recall for the other disciples how their hearts were burning within them when they listened to Jesus' words of healing and hope.

Each of us has already begun our grief journey—sometimes for more than one loved one at a time. We begin it by telling our own story, but it continues when we listen to the Lord. Through prayer we will hear his voice. Prayer is taking the time to slow down our lives so that we may hear God talking to us. We don't need to multiply our recitation of formal prayers to do this. As Jesus taught us, "your Father knows what you need before you ask him" (Matthew 6:8).

The Lord has much to say to us and to show us in our grief. He comes to us having suffered loss and death himself. He comes to us in understanding, gentleness, peace, love, support and strength. Prayer is sometimes hard when we are mourning the loss of a loved one. Somehow the words can stick in our throat. But a prayer of listening can be healing, quiet and growth-filled. It can help us move along the last few miles on the road from Jerusalem to Emmaus and allow us to recognize and pay attention to the stranger who approaches us on that road. It can leave our hearts "burning within us."

QUESTIONS

As you continue along your grief journey, you will continue to have ups and downs, doubts and fears. God is with you on your journey. All you need do is listen. Try to write down a few thoughts on the following questions in the space provided. Share your answers with someone else when and if you can.

How do you relate to Jesus' experience in the Garden of Gethsemane?

Have you walked far enough on your grief journey to be able to listen to God? What have you begun to hear?

How would you respond to someone (or yourself) who says, "I'm too upset to pray" or "God has not heard my prayers"?

What do you think the disciples on the road to Emmaus experienced when their "hearts were burning" inside them?

Have you had a similar experience on your grief journey? Describe it.

When will you be able to walk with others on their grief journeys? How will you begin?

A Call to Journey beyond Loss

"She died too young," Tim cried. "My little daughter Mary was only three years old. She should not have died. There is nothing left for me now."

"I thought we would be married and live together forever," Peg sobbed. "Now that my husband Jim has died, life doesn't mean a thing to me."

Tim and Peg and more people than we can count have experienced the loss of a loved one. Through that death, life has seemed to come to an end for them, too. They are discouraged, fearful, unhappy, lonely. They have lost the meaning in their lives.

But others who have suffered like Tim and Peg have somehow found a way to turn their pain and loss into instruments to build up their faith and hope. Their losses eventually have made them rely not on themselves, but on God. They recognize that they are powerless, but in that recognition comes the strength to move on in their grief journey. They do so with complete trust and dependence on God, rather than on themselves.

The journey we travel after the loss of a loved one can become a journey toward new life. That's hard for us to hear when we are in the very beginnings of our grief. Spirituality is probably the farthest thing from our minds. Our emotions have been ripped raw. We are suffering and in great pain.

"I don't want to pray," Susan screamed. "I can't! How could God take Bill from me?"

"How will I ever be able to talk with God again?" Tim asked angrily.

Yet Susan and Tim expressed those feelings on a weekend retreat that they had come to months after the death of her husband and his daughter. They somehow knew that they needed to "spend some time with the Lord," as Susan put it.

They said they couldn't pray, and yet they had willingly come to a place where praying was the order of the day. Somehow, without even realizing it, Susan and Tim had experienced an inner call to move on their grief journeys to a power that lay beyond themselves.

The story of the Annunciation can teach us how it is possible to move from grief to grace. Mary was called upon to face the impossible: "How can this be, since I am a virgin?" (Luke 1:34). She would lose all that she had hoped for: a peaceful life with Joseph, the love and respect of her family and friends and neighbors.

Mary could have said, "No, you are asking too much," but instead she said, "Here I am, the servant of the Lord; let it be with me according to your word" (Luke 1:38). Her response to being asked to do the impossible was to trust in God and begin a journey that would take her beyond her losses to new life. Her leap of faith, her unequivocal "yes" to the impossible, not only enriched and enlivened Mary, but it has resounded through all the ages.

It is that same leap of faith that God is asking all of us to take. "Blessed are those who mourn" (Matthew 5:4), Jesus promised us. Yes, we are being asked to do the impossible, but nothing is impossible with God.

"My precious child, I love you and I would never leave you."

Where are you now on your grief journey? On the next two pages, describe where you have been, what you think lies ahead, and how you have experienced God with you. If you prefer to type or need more room, use additional pages and attach them to the book.

_____

_____

_____

_____

_____

_____

_____

_____

_____

_____

_____

_____

_____

_____

_____

_____

_____

_____

_____

_____

_____

_____

_____

_____

CLOSING PRAYER

Pray the "Serenity Prayer" found on p. 84 of this book.

Moving toward Closure

PRAYER

The Lord is my shepherd,
I shall not want.

He makes me lie down
in green pastures.

He leads me beside still waters;
he restores my soul.

He leads me in right paths
for his name's sake.

Even though I walk through the darkest valley,
I fear no evil.

For you are with me;
your rod and your staff–they comfort me.

Psalm 23:1-4

Additional selections from Scripture:
- Luke 23:33, 39-43
- John 16:20-14
- Colossians 4:1-4

REFLECTION

Saying Good-bye and Saying Hello

All growth is saying good-bye and saying hello. We say good-bye to the womb before saying hello to the world. We say good-bye to childhood before saying hello to the adult experience. We say good-bye to the past before saying hello to the future.

Good-byes do not have to be said in anger. They do not have to be said in hurt. But they must be said, even though it is never pleasant to do so.

The most painful good-bye is the one we say to a loved one after his or her death. No one can prepare us for this good-bye, but even it can lead to a hello—a hello to growth.

Life is not supposed to stop with the death of a loved one. We know that by now. We are to continue living, in fact we are to continue growing. We do not know why we have been called to face our grief, but one thing we can be sure of is that we are not made to do so as a punishment. God does not parlay one life against another or take one life to punish another life.

Nor did the death of our loved one occur so that we could grow. But growth can come from the event, if we do not take the death as a sentence to a life of sadness or loneliness.

We have many new experiences ahead of us. We have new worlds to explore, new feelings to feel, new relationships to develop. None of this will come easily or quickly. We will crawl before we walk. It is like beginning a whole new life all over again. But it can happen.

We need to give ourselves permission to say good-bye so that we can say hello. The life ahead of us is uncharted and uncertain, but it is to be lived to the fullest. God is calling us to journey toward new life, and he has promised that he will be with us on it.

(For further reading on this topic, see *Don't Take My Grief Away* by Doug Manning.)

QUESTIONS

As you seek closure on this stage of your grief journey, reflect on how far you have come and where you still need to go. Try to write down a few thoughts on the following questions in the space provided. Share your answers with someone else when and if you can.

Recall your initial feelings after the loss of your loved one. How have they changed?

What issues do you still need to deal with? How will you do so?

Have you found journaling to be helpful? Why?

Do you want to continue to reflect on your grief? How can you do so?

What are the good-byes you still need to make? When and how will you do so?

What are some of the new things that you must say hello to?

Setting Realistic Goals

We all have goals, but some of us are more successful at accomplishing them than others. When the issue is overcoming our grief and moving on, setting realistic goals is even more difficult than usual, because of the emotions involved.

Here are some suggestions to help you set and achieve your goals on your grief journey:

1. List the things you want to accomplish in the time line you have given yourself. Ask yourself these questions: Are these really your goals? Are they worth the trouble? How will you know when you have reached a particular goal? Are the goals possible given your schedule, finances, talents, and even opposition from others? Make sure your goals are clear, specific, measurable and worth doing.

2. Organize your goals for each time period in the order of their importance.

3. Work out specific things you can do to achieve your goals. Talk to others and don't be afraid to ask for their help.

4. Choose those goals that can be started on immediately and have the best chance for success in a short amount of time. (It may be necessary to put off some of your most important goals until you have more time or are better able to address them.)

5. When you have written down your goals, put them in some kind of "tickler" file—some place that you will be sure to review them in a timely manner. (For example, tape them to your bathroom mirror or staple them in your appointment book or calendar.)

If you follow this advice, you will begin to accomplish some of your goals. Then you can set other—perhaps more ambitious—goals, until finally one day you will look up and be amazed by how far you have journeyed.

"The Lord is my shepherd, I shall not want."

Now is the time for closure on this part of your grief journey. On the next three pages, describe some goals for your life as you'd like it to be right now, three months from now, and a year from now. If you prefer to type or need more room, use additional pages and attach them to the book.

Goals for Now

_____

_____

_____

_____

_____

_____

_____

_____

_____

_____

Goals for Three Months from Now

_____

_____

_____

_____

_____

_____

_____

_____

_____

_____

_____

_____

_____

Goals for a Year from Now

_____

_____

_____

_____

_____

_____

_____

_____

_____

_____

_____

_____

CLOSING PRAYER

Pray the "Serenity Prayer" found on p. 84 of this book.

APPENDIXES

Journaling around the Holidays

Suggestions for Further Reading

Bereavement Support Groups

Prayers for the Bereaved

Facilitator's Guide

Acknowledgements

JOURNALING AROUND THE HOLIDAYS

Holidays can be an especially difficult time for those who grieve. There
is much focus on family and friends, everyone is in a festive spirit,
there are many special (and often tiring) activities, and the memories of
sharing previous holidays with a deceased loved one can be especially
strong. Celebrating the holidays will be different for you now than it
has been in the past, and it might be helpful to focus on how to move
through the stress of these times by doing some journaling.

On these two pages, describe how you celebrated holidays with your loved one in
previous years and how and with whom you will celebrate this year. Look at your past
holiday customs and traditions and see which you want to retain and which you want to
change. If you prefer to type or need more room, use additional pages and attach them
to the book.

_____

_____

_____

_____

_____

_____

_____

_____

Suggestions for Further Reading

General

Don't Take My Grief Away from Me, Doug Manning, InSight Books, 1979.

The Tree That Survived the Winter, Mary Fahy, Paulist Press, 1989.

What Helped Me When My Loved One Died, edited by Earl Grollman, Beacon Press, 1981.

When Bad Things Happen to Good People, Rabbi Harold Kushner, Avon Books, 1981.

Spirituality/Prayer

Blessed Grieving, Joan Guntzelman, St. Mary's Press, 1994

From Grief to Grace, Helen Reichert Lambin, ACTA Publications, 1994.

Praying Our Goodbyes, Joyce Rupp, Ave Maria Press, 1988.

Praying Through Grief: Healing Prayer Services for Those Who Mourn, Mauryeen O'Brien, Ave Maria Press, 1997.

Psalms for Times of Trouble, John Carmody, Twenty-Third Publications, 1995.

Death of a Spouse

The Death of a Husband, Helen Reichert Lambin, ACTA Publications, 1997

The Death of a Wife, Robert L. Vogt, ACTA Publications, 1996.

When Your Spouse Dies, Cathleen Curry, Ave Maria Press, 1998.

Death of a Parent

Finding Your Way, Richard Gilbert, Ave Maria Press, 1999.

Motherless Daughters, Hope Edelman, Dell Publishing, 1995.

When Your Parent Dies, Cathleen Curry, Ave Maria Press, 1993.

Death of a Child

Always Precious in Our Memory, Kristen Johnson Ingram, ACTA Publications, 1998.

Dear Parents, edited by Joy Johnson, Centering Corporation, 1999.

Empty Arms, Sherokee Ilse, Wintergreen Press, 1992.

Death through Suicide

My Son...My Son, Iris Bolton, Bolton Press, 1983.

Suicide: Prevention, Intervention, Postvention, Earl Grollman, Beacon Press, 1971.

Children's Books

The Fall of Freddy the Leaf, Leo Buscaglia, Holt, Reinhart and Winston, 1982.

Hope for the Flowers, Trina Paulus, Paulist Press, 1972.

"Love, Mark," Mark Scrivani, Hope for Bereaved, 1986.

A Taste of Blackberries, Doris B. Smith, Scholastic Book Services, 1976.

"Helping" Books

Grief Counseling and Grief Therapy, Second Edition, J. William Worden, Springer Publishing Company, 1991.

No Time for Goodbyes, Janice Harris Lord, Pathfinder, 1987.

On Children and Death, Elisabeth Kubler-Ross, MacMillan Publishing, 1983.

Understanding Grief, Alan D. Wolfelt, Accelerated Development Publishers, 1992.

Magazines and Newsletters

Bereavement, Bereavement Publishing, (719-266-0006).

Journey, National Catholic Ministry to the Bereaved, (440-943-3480).

Healing Ministry, Prime National Publishing, (781-899-2702).

BEREAVEMENT SUPPORT GROUPS

"The funeral has been over for six months, and everyone I meet either tells me I should be better–or at least their eyes imply it," Jane said to me when we met outside of church one warm summer morning.

"I know it's been a while," she cried, "but I don't feel better. What's worse, I don't know what to do about it. I need to talk to someone who knows what I'm going through."

Indeed, Jane is right. She knows her emotions very well. But she is also in touch with what she truly needs–someone with whom to share her feelings, someone who has experienced the death of a loved one and knows what she is going through.

Who can understand the grief, loneliness, and questioning of a bereaved person better than someone who has suffered a similar loss? Here is peer ministry in its highest form: those who have experienced the loss of a loved one sharing their own pain with others in like circumstances in an effort to provide a means by which healing can take place for both of them.

So the concept of a "bereavement support group" was born. It provides the opportunity for a grieving person to be listened to, understood, nurtured, and loved. Although it is not a "therapy" group, it can be growth producing. It is not an "answer" group but rather a "question" group, where there are no wrong questions and no easy answers. The answers come from the people in the group who have experienced grief.

For example, when Jane asks, "How long is it going to take me to feel better?" she won't receive a pat response from a support group. Instead, she will hear the lived experience of a Monica or a Richard or a Zack. Each one had to make his or her own grief journey and knows what Jane is going through. She will get many different answers to that one heart-rending question, and one of them will strike a chord. Jane will see a similarity, a response to her needs, a permission to live within her own unique rhythms.

Is a support group the only avenue you should take? No, it is just one more way to get help in moving through your grief. But it has been proven that those who have suffered the loss of a loved one can share their experiences and be nurtured in a loving and caring community. That sense of community is extremely important to those who feel disconnected and alone in their grief, and it is the foundation of Christian life.

If you feel the need to have others walk beside you on your grief journey, you might want to consider joining or even helping to form a bereavement support group. Sharing your grief can often help to diminish it.

PRAYERS FOR THE BEREAVED

SERENITY PRAYER

God, grant me the serenity

to accept the things I cannot change,

the courage to change the things I can,

and the wisdom to know the difference.

Living one day at a time,

enjoying one moment at a time,

accepting hardship as a pathway to peace,

taking, as Jesus did,

this sinful world as it is,

not as I would have it,

trusting that you will make all things right

if I surrender to your will,

so that I may be reasonably happy in this life

and supremely happy with you forever in the next.

Amen.

A PRAYER OF BLESSING FOR ALL WHO GRIEVE

May the God of strength be with you and keep you in strong-fingered hands; may you be the sacrament of strength to those entrusted to your care.

May the blessing of strength be upon you.

May the God of mercy be with you, forgiving you, beckoning you, encouraging you to say "I will get up again and go to my Father's house;" may your readiness to forgive calm the fear of those who hurt you.

May the blessing of mercy be upon you.

May the God of wonder be with you, delighting you with thunder and wind, sunrise and rain—enchanting your senses, filling your heart, opening your eyes to the splendor of creation; and may you open the hands, eyes, and hearts of the blind and insensitive.

May the blessing of wonder be upon you.

May the God of simplicity be with you, opening you to a clear vision of truth, leading you deeply into the mystery of childhood; and may your dealings with others be marked by the honesty that is simplicity.

May the blessing of simplicity be on you.

May the God of patience be with you, waiting for you with outstretched arms, letting you find out for yourself; may you be patient with the young who fall from small heights, and the old who fall from greater heights.

May the blessing of patience be upon you.

May the God of peace be with you, stilling the heart that hammers with fear, doubt and confusion; and may the warm mantle of your peace cover the anxious.

May the blessing of peace be upon you.

May the God of love be with you, drawing you close; may this love in you be for those you serve; may this love glow in your eyes and meet God's love reflected in the eyes of your friends.

May the blessing of love be upon you.

Amen.

WITH YOUR MORNING, THEN, WILL MY MOURNING END

Lord, you have taken.

My loss with languor fills me, and drains me
as swiftly as the fleet departure of an ocean eventide

I did not watch, tonight, the sunset flush or fade
while an artist nearby presented on canvas
its resplendent moment in Time—the craft-work of Thine—
radiant to him in hues of burgundy wine.

No. My head was hung in mourning my loss.
Now, in the night, I still mourn.
T'was your will, Lord, for me to have loved and to lose my Love.
How can I fathom your Giving and Taking?

What drives you to weave, with brushstrokes of your whim,
a sunset engorged in red-laden layers
from the easel of your will—to last just a breath of a moment—
then to dash your masterpieces into the depth of the sea?
Why do you Send and Remove?

"What is dearer to heart," you answered,
"the crimson rose whose stem was raised from my earth,
or the rose of cloth petals, spun by machine?
Yet, which rose endures...and which one must die?
Which could be given, then given away,
and which—but once—would be Gift?

This came to me, then:
The artist's sunset-artificial of chemical on canvas
will grace someone's living room wall for life,
but the genuine print from your hand, Lord,
was the worthier Gift made precious by its brevity.
So it is with my Love and my loving.

Soon morning. Soon sunrise.
Shall I raise to the east my eyes to receive its pastel glories
and accept my lost Love for what it really was—
the worthiest Gift of all from you to me?
With your morning, then, will my mourning end.

Look now. The warmth of your new sun
spills over my face and dries my tears and brightens my memories
and I smile at the promise of a New Day.

Lord, you have given.

(From *A Mortal on the Mend)*

PRAYER OF THE BEREAVED

We give our loved ones back to you, Lord,
as you gave them to us.

As you did not lose in the giving,
neither do we lose them in the return.

What you give,
you never really take away.

What is yours is always ours also,
if we are yours.

Life is eternal, Lord,
and your love is undying.

Death is only a horizon,
and a horizon is nothing but the limits of our
sight.

Lift us up, strong Son of God,
on that same cross on which you were raised,
so that we may see farther.

Open our eyes,
as you opened the eyes of the man born blind,
so that we may see more clearly.

Draw us closer to yourself,
as you drew the little children to you,
so that we may be closer to our loved ones
who are with you.

While you prepare a place for them,
prepare us to live without them for a while.

Amen.

RITE OF PASSAGE

Father,
I once knelt before you
piece by piece
in dire need to lean on you.
I prayed for you to fix me
You didn't
I was still in pieces
so
feeling all alone
I decided to fix myself
I'm here, today,
before you
my pieces all together
I made myself stand up again.

Thank you, Father,
for giving me what I really needed;
the will, at last,
to cause myself to heal,
the courage to stand
alone
and the wisdom
to know that I never was.

Amen.

(From *A Mortal on the Mend*)

MEMORIAL LIGHT SERVICE

(This prayer service can be performed alone or with others.)

Heavenly Father, I am on a very difficult journey. I have struggled to face the death of my loved one, a task that has left me grieving and questioning, lonely and sometimes afraid.

But with your love, I have been able to begin this journey. I know it isn't over and that I will still grieve. Be with me as I continue it.

I try, now, to memorialize my loved one in my memory and heart with this service of light.

(Light a candle.)

I light this candle in remembrance of my loved one who has died but now lives with the resurrected Christ. Lord, you are the light of the world. Shed that light on me and let it be a reminder that my loved one enjoys eternal light and happiness with you.

Amen.

PRAYER FOR REUNION

Father of mercies and God of all consolation,
you pursue us with untiring love
and dispel the shadow of death
with the bright dawn of life.

Your Son, our Lord Jesus Christ,
by dying has destroyed our death,
and by rising, restored our life.
Enable us therefore to press on toward him,
so that, after our earthly course is run,
he may reunite us with those we love,
when every tear will be wiped away.

We ask this through Christ our Lord.

Amen.

(From the *Order of Christian Funerals*)

FACILITATOR'S GUIDE

This guide is for people who are facilitating a bereavement support group using *The New Day Journal*. It is important that facilitators have already worked through the grief process for themselves. There needs to be at least one facilitator for each eight people in the group. If there is more than one facilitator, one person needs to be the program leader.

INTRODUCTION

Your role as a facilitator is simply to make the journey through grief an easier one for those suffering from the loss of a loved one. Although your role is important, it is limited. You are most likely not a professional counselor, psychologist, or psychiatrist. If any of the participants in the group exhibit or express the need for professional help, you need to make an immediate referral. (Prior to the first session, make sure that you have acquired the names and phone numbers of professional therapists who are ready and willing to accept new clients.)

Remember that it is important for you as the facilitator to also nurture yourself as you begin to help others. Set up a feedback system with other facilitators or people in ministry. Set limits on your availability to group members so that you don't run the risk of burn-out yourself or build dependencies on the part of people in your group.

OUTLINE OF BOOK

The New Day Journal is divided into Part One, "The Four Tasks of Grief, and Part Two, "Continuing the Grief Journey." There are seven sessions in Part One and two sessions in Part Two. These should be held over nine consecutive weeks. The Appendix also has a section for special journaling during the holiday season, information for people to read on bereavement support groups, and suggestions for further reading on grief. Also included are prayers for people who are grieving, which you can substitute for suggested prayers, recommend that people pray on their own, or use in any other way you see fit.

PREPARING THE ENVIRONMENT

The meetings of the group can be held in a comfortable room in a church or rectory or in someone's home. They should be held at the same time and place each week, because people in the grieving process need as much structure in their lives as possible. The room should be small enough to allow for intimacy, but large enough to accommodate everyone and have space to break out into small groups if there are nine people or more.

You are encouraged to play soft, instrumental music before each session begins and anytime you feel silent reflection time is needed. Here are some recommended songs: *Turn to Me, Only in God,* and *The Cry of the Poor* by John Foley; *On Eagles Wings, I Have Loved You,* and *Be Not Afraid* by Michael Joncas; *Come to Me All You Who Are Weary* and *Here I Am, Lord* by Dan Schutte. Recordings of these songs are all available from GIA Publications, 7404 S. Mason Avenue, Chicago, IL 60638, 800-442-1358.

You might want to have refreshments available as people come in and have a refreshment break during each session. It is not important that these refreshments be elaborate or costly.

SUGGESTED FORMAT

It is recommended that each session follow a predictable pattern and last approximately the same amount of time. Here is an outline for a two-hour session:

Introduction/Prayer—5 minutes

> Call everyone together while music is playing in the background. Introduce yourself and any co-facilitators, then have each participant introduce themselves and tell why they have come. Tell people that the purpose of this program is to bring together people who have suffered a significant loss in their lives. Remind them that it is necessary and healthy to mourn or grieve the death of a loved one and that it is often helpful to share and work through the tasks of grief together.

> Explain the importance of listening and confidentiality and letting everyone have the opportunity to share.

> Then begin the session by having someone read the prayer for the session or use one of the "Additional Selections from Scripture."

Sharing of Journal Entries—10 minutes

> In the first session, read aloud or have people read to themselves the short essay on journal writing in the front of the book. In the following sessions, invite the participants to share one or two entries from their journal writing with others in the large group. Everyone should feel welcome to share, but no one should be required to do so.

Reading/Reflection—20 minutes

> Read aloud or have the participants read to themselves the "Reflection" for the session. Leave time for silent reflection on the reading. Invite anyone who has a comment on the reflection to do so in the large group.

Questions—15 minutes

> Have people briefly write their answers to the six "Questions" in the book.

Small Group Discussion—45 minutes

> If there are nine people or more, break into groups of 4-8 people each. You need one facilitator for each small group. Otherwise, stay in the large group. Discuss the participants' answers to the questions.

Large Group Sharing—15 minutes

> If you formed small groups, bring everyone back to a large group and ask the facilitators to share important points that were made in the small group discussions. Allow participants to comment.

Assignment—5 minutes

> Encourage people to do the "Reading" and "Journaling" in the book before the next session. Impress upon them that the work done between the sessions is as important as what happens in the group.

Closing Prayer/Announcements—5 minutes

> Have everyone read aloud the *Serenity Prayer* found on p. 84 of the book.

> Finally, give the number, dates, times, and places of the remaining sessions. Pass around a list asking new participants for their names, addresses, phone numbers and the anniversary dates of the death of their loved one. (These anniversary dates can be noted in the prayer times of the appropriate sessions.)

> End by inviting people to stay for refreshments and talk informally.

END OF THE LAST SESSION

At the end of the very last session of the group, you should plan time to summarize what the group has done and to celebrate a special prayer service. You might begin be saying something like this:

"We have been meeting now for many weeks, and today we are celebrating the end of one thing and the beginning of something else. We have gotten to know each other in ways that few people do. We have learned to accept and trust each other and to be vulnerable in ways we did not think possible. We have let go of a lot of pain and come to embrace our futures. I have watched each of you grow in self-confidence as you ministered to others in the group. I have also noticed unique qualities in each of you that show me that you have the capacity to heal from your grief."

You might then identify a quality you have noticed in each member of the group. If you have had co-facilitators, you might let them do this.

Then read or have one of the participants read the *Rite of Passage* prayer on p. 87 of this book. Then conduct the *Memorial Light Service* found on p. 88. (Note: This service can also be substituted for the *Serenity Prayer* at the end of any or all of the regular sessions.)

End the session with this blessing:

"May you feel the power of this small community of people who love you as you continue to heal and grow after the death of your loved one. Our thoughts, prayers and love will always be part of your new life and will give you strength for your journey. Amen."

Suggest that participants continue their journaling, especially around the holidays, and consider further reading from the list in the book. Finally, announce that it is a good idea for the group to come back together after three months for a reunion to see how each person is progressing on their grief journey. Have the group schedule the reunion, but be sure to remind everyone by mail and/or phone when the time comes. (Some participants may opt to not come to the reunion, and they should not be pressured to do so.)

There may be strong feelings among the group at the end of the sessions. Some participants may express concern that they need the group to continue. Point them toward the reunion and assure them that they are progressing well. If necessary, suggest that they consider repeating the program with a new group.

Encourage people to stay for refreshments and informal sharing. Ask each participant to fill out an evaluation form before they leave.

REUNION

The reunion can be a very informal affair of one to two hours. Refreshments should be served, and some groups even have a "potluck" meal. Participants should be encouraged to share from their journals where they have been and where they are now on their grief journey. For most people, there has been a lot of progress. Those who are still "stuck" in their grief will be encouraged that things will get better.

It can also be suggested at this time that participants consider repeating the nine sessions with a new group, both to help themselves continue their grief work and to begin to help others. (Many people who have gone through this program more than once make excellent facilitators for future groups.)

Finally, you can repeat all or part of the summary and prayer service used at the end of the last session.

EVALUATION

At the end of the last session, participants should be asked to complete a simple evaluation form. The facilitators should then meet within a week to review the answers, to make their own evaluation of the sessions, to support each other, and to plan for further sessions based on the feedback.

Sample evaluation questions:

1. What did you hope to gain from this program?

2. How have these expectations been met or not met?

3. Would you change anything about this program? Please be specific in your suggestions.

CONCLUSION

Facilitating the grieving process of others can be both a difficult and a rewarding experience. It is important that you remember several things:

• You are grieving yourself, for grieving is part of the human condition.

• You cannot do people's grief work for them or make their lives better. You can only encourage them to do it for themselves.

• You cannot do this alone. You need a team or colleagues with whom to share what you are going through.

• You will be rewarded for your effort with the gratitude of others and your own growth.

God bless you.

ACKNOWLEDGMENTS

My special thanks to Dr. J. William Worden, author of *Grief Counseling and Grief Therapy*, upon whose work this book is based, and to Vincent Marquis, author of *A Mortal on the Mend*, whose poetry is found in the prayer section.

I am grateful to Cecilia O'Brien and Donald Pyers for their contributions to the assembly of this text and to the first facilitators of the New Day seminars, who piloted the program and evaluated the material: Rose DeJager, Kenneth Stanton, Marie Esposito, Noreen Pintarich, Philip Gravel, Andrew Porto, Carmella Jameson and Mary Ann Zelek.

Special acknowledgment is made to Carmel Avitabile and Eleanore Boruch, who have facilitated many New Day groups and continue to aid in the training of New Day facilitators.

Thanks to the Catholic Cemeteries Association, the Archdiocese of Hartford, D'Esopo Funeral Chapel in Wethersfield, Connecticut and the Newkirk and Whitney Funeral Home in East Hartford for their special support of the New Day program.

Finally, thanks to Gregory Pierce of ACTA Publications for his constant encouragement and tireless editing of this revision of *The New Day Journal*.

Every effort has been made to determine ownership of all texts that have been quoted or adapted and to make arrangements for their use. Any oversights that may have occurred will be corrected in future editions.

ADDITIONAL GRIEF RESOURCES
FROM ACTA PUBLICATIONS

Lift Up Your Hearts
Meditations for Those Who Mourn
MAURYEEN O'BRIEN, OP

Over forty complete personal prayer experiences by Sr. Maruyeen O'Brien, author of the *New Day Journal,* are designed to help those in mourning pass prayerfully through the four tasks of grief (Accept the Reality, Experience the Pain, Adjust to Change, Create Memories and Goals). Psalm verses and scripture passages combined with reflections, questions and prayers connect a grieving person with the spirit of the healing Lord. (112-page paperback, $8.95)

Hidden Presence
Twelve Blessings That Transformed
Sorrow or Loss
EDITED BY GREGORY F. AUGUSTINE PIERCE

A collection of true stories of blessings that somehow transformed a sorrow or loss. Each of the twelve storytellers in this book recalls a very real benefit or insight gained from a tragedy, failure, illness or disaster in his or her life. (176-page hardcover gift book with silver ribbon, $17.95)

The Death of a Child
Reflections for Grieving Parents
ELAINE STILLWELL

Written by a well-known bereavement minister who lost two children in a car accident, this new book explores the steps parents need to take to grieve their child's death and then somehow find the way to continue on with life themselves. (128-page paperback, $9.95)

The Death of a Parent
Reflections for Adults Mourning the Loss
of a Father or Mother
DELLE CHATMAN
WITH MEDITATIONS BY REV. WILLIAM KENNEALLY

Filled with stories of people who have lost a parent and how they dealt with the reality of that event. A spiritual reflection concludes each of the sections. (128-page paperback, $9.95)

The Death of a Husband
Reflections for a Grieving Wife
HELEN REICHERT LAMBIN

Over forty reflections offer insights that will touch a woman's heart, heal her soul, and point out new and hopeful directions. (128-page paperback, $9.95)

The Death of a Wife
Reflections for a Grieving Husband
ROBERT VOGT

Each of these 31 brief reflections, remembrances, stories and meditations considers a different facet of the grieving process for husbands. (112-page paperback, $9.95)

Tear Soup
A Recipe for Healing after Loss
PAT SCHWIEBERT AND CHUCK DeKLYEN
ILLUSTRATED BY TAYLOR BILLS

Voted the best children's book of 2001 by the Association of Theological Booksellers, this modern-day fable tells the story of a woman who has suffered a terrible loss and must cook up a special batch of "tear soup" in order to grieve. Richly illustrated, for children and adults alike. (56-page hardcover gift book, $19.95)

From Grief to Grace
Images for Overcoming Sadness and Loss
HELEN R. LAMBIN

A collection of images that assist people in naming, processing and overcoming grief caused by illness, a loved one's death, a job loss or similar difficult situations. (96-page paperback, $8.95)

Available from booksellers or call 800-397-2282
www.actapublications.com